JAN - - 2015

Cougar

A Cat with Many Names

by Stephen Person

Consultant: Clayton K. Nielsen, PhD
Associate Professor of Forest Wildlife, Cooperative Wildlife Research Laboratory
Department of Forestry, Center for Ecology, Southern Illinois University Carbondale;
Director of Scientific Research, The Cougar Network

BEARPORT PUBLISHING

New York, New York

Credits

Cover and Title Page, © Dennis Donohue/Shutterstock; 4, © age fotostock/SuperStock; 5, © Courtesy of Gail Loveman; 6, © Granier Laurent/Alamy; 6 7,© Norbert Rosing/National Geographic/Getty Images; 7, © age fotostock/SuperStock; 8, © Oregon Historical Society bb009230; 10,© Corbis/SuperStock; 11, © Ronald Wittek/dpa/Landov; 12T, © Animals Animals/SuperStock; 12B, © Tom & Pat Leeson; 13B, © Minden Pictures/SuperStock; 13T, © Thomas Kitchin & Victoria Hurst/First Light/Getty Images; 14, © Animals Animals/SuperStock; 15T, © Tom & Pat Leeson; 15B, © imagebroker/SuperStock; 16T, © Daniel J Cox/Oxford Scientific/Getty Images; 16B, © Dennis Fast/VWPics/SuperStock; 17, © age fotostock/SuperStock; 18, © Daniel J Cox/Oxford Scientific/Getty Images; 19, © Gerard Lacz/age fotostock/SuperStock; 20, © Courtesy of Lue and Krystal Vang; 21T, © Reuters/Landov; 21B, © Altrendo/Getty Images; 22, © A & C Wiley/Wales/Photolibrary/Getty Images; 23, © mlorenz/Shutterstock; 24, © Erwin & Peggy Bauer/Wildstock; 25, © Stuart Westmorland/Photo Researchers/Getty Images; 26, © Clyde Mueller/The New Mexican; 27, © Tier und Naturfotografie/SuperStock; 28, © Biosphoto/J. L. Klein & M. L. Hubert; 29,© Kenneth Delahunt.

Publisher: Kenn Goin
Editorial Director: Adam Siegel
Creative Director: Spencer Brinker
Design: Dawn Beard Creative
Photo Researcher: Picture Perfect Professionals, LLC

Library of Congress Cataloging in Publication Data

Person, Stephen.
  Cougar : a cat with many names / by Stephen Person.
    p. cm. — (America's hidden animal treasures)
  Includes bibliographical references and index.
  ISBN 978 1 61772 569 2 (library binding) — ISBN 1 61772 569 2 (library binding)
  1. Puma—Juvenile literature. I. Title.
  QL737.C23P423 2013
  599.75'24—dc23

                          2012003342

For more information, write to Bearport Publishing Company, Inc., 45 West 21st Street, Suite 3B, New York, New York 10010. Printed in the United States of America.

10 9 8 7 6 5 4

Contents

Zeus and the Cougar

Early one evening in October 2011, Gail Loveman heard a strange grumbling noise coming from outside her house in Boulder, Colorado. She looked through the glass door leading to her backyard—and was shocked by what she saw. There, standing on her porch, was a cougar!

Cougars are sometimes called the "cat of many names." In addition to *cougar*, this animal is known as mountain lion, panther, painter, puma, catamount, and has more than 30 other names.

Gail was not the only one who wanted to see the unusual visitor. Gail's cat, Zeus, padded up to the glass door for a closer look. "I think he thought, 'Hmm, this is different!'" Gail said of her curious cat. For about five minutes, Zeus and the cougar stood just inches apart, staring at each other through the glass. Finally, the cougar turned, jumped over a fence, and headed out of sight.

Habitat All Around

It's not every day that a cougar walks right up to a home in Boulder. "People can live there their entire lives and not see them," says Jennifer Churchill of the Colorado Division of Wildlife. Still, **biologists** know that cougars roam the mountains near Boulder—and many other places as well.

Cougars live in many habitats, including this Arizona desert.

WARNING / CAUTION
MOUNTAIN LION

MOUNTAIN LIONS HAVE BEEN SPOTTED NEAR THE TRAILS.

DO NOT
UNDER ANY CIRCUMSTANCE
ALLOW SMALL CHILDREN
TO WANDER OR RUN
OFF ALONE WHILE
IN THE PRESERVE

Signs like this one teach people how to stay safe when hiking in areas where cougars have been seen.

People rarely meet a cougar in the wild. If they do, however, they should make loud noises and try to appear as big as possible. This can help convince the wild cat not to attack. Most important, people should not try to run away. Running can trigger the cougar's **instinct** to chase and hunt.

In fact, cougars have an amazing ability to **adapt** to almost any type of **habitat**. The big cats are fast and powerful. They can swim, climb trees, and jump up to 15 feet (4.6 m) high. All of these skills, along with their sharp eyesight and **keen** hearing, make them excellent hunters that can adapt to life in mountains, forests, deserts, plains, and wetlands.

Cougars can reach a speed of 50 miles per hour (80 kph) in short sprints. That's much faster than any human can run.

People and Cougars

If cougars can adapt to so many different types of habitat, why don't they live everywhere in North America? The answer is, they used to—except in the northern most parts. When European **settlers** arrived about 400 years ago, cougars could be found in many areas of Canada and almost every part of what is now the United States. As the human **population** increased, however, people and cougars **competed** for the same areas.

In the 1800s and early 1900s, many states paid hunters for each cougar they killed. These rewards caused cougar populations all over the United States to fall.

Settlers wanted more land to build farms and towns. As farmers moved into the areas where cougars lived, they worried that the wild cats would eat their **livestock**. As a result, people started hunting cougars. They killed so many that by the early 1800s, the animals were nearly wiped out in the eastern half of the United States. In the West, where there is more wilderness, the cougars were not in danger of dying out. They survived in areas that were not settled by people.

Cougars in the Wild

It is still legal to hunt cougars today in western states where their populations are **stable**. Most of these states limit the number of cougars hunters can kill, hoping to keep cougar populations from getting too low.

☐ Where cougars live

Cougars can be found from Canada to the tip of South America.

Secretive Cats

Today, the cougar population of the United States is **estimated** to be 30,000. Nearly all of the wild cats live in western states. Even when cougars live near cities such as Boulder, however, it's rare for people to see them. That's because cougars are **solitary** animals and avoid contact with humans. For most of their lives, cougars even avoid other cougars. Each adult animal lives alone within its own large **territory**.

When it is time to **mate**, male and female cougars come together, usually at the edges of their territories.

How much territory does a cougar need? The exact amount depends on the type of habitat, but at least ten square miles (26 sq km) is necessary. Each cougar needs a territory with enough water to drink and enough **prey** to hunt. In the deserts of west Texas, for example, water and prey are **scarce**—so cougar territories can be as large as 1,000 square miles (2,590 sq km).

Cougars are very good at climbing trees. This allows them to get away from humans, bears, or packs of wolves.

Going in for the Kill

No matter where cougars live, they need to be able to hunt to stay alive—and these big cats are expert **predators**. Deer is the cougars' favorite prey, but the wild cats will hunt almost any animal they can find. They catch and eat wild hogs, elk, bighorn sheep, coyotes, rabbits, raccoons, birds, and even porcupines.

A cougar chasing a bighorn sheep

Sometimes a cougar will climb a tree to catch a porcupine.

Cougars have to be careful when battling strong prey such as deer, elk, or bighorn sheep. The wild cats can be kicked, stabbed with horns, or tossed onto sharp rocks by the powerful animals. If a cougar's back or leg gets broken, it will be unable to hunt and may starve to death.

When cougars spot their prey, they follow silently behind. Then they pounce on the animal, killing it with a powerful bite to the neck. After eating some of the meat, cougars will often cover the **carcass** with leaves or grass to hide it from other hungry animals. This way, the cougar can return to feed on the rest of the meat over the next several days.

Cougars use their large, sharp teeth to catch and kill prey.

This cougar is covering an elk it has killed so that other animals will be less likely to find it and eat it.

Mothers and Kittens

While all cougars hunt in the same way, the lives of male and female cougars are very different. When female cougars reach the age of about two and a half, they are old enough to have young. After mating, a female cougar gives birth in a **den** to a **litter** of two or three kittens. The father does not help raise the young—the mother must do the job herself.

For about two months, a cougar mother hides her kittens from predators by keeping them in a den. A den may be between a pile of rocks, in a cave, or under the low branches of a tree.

Mother cougars **nurse** their kittens for about two months. After that, the young cougars are strong enough to leave the den and begin following their mother around her territory. They can now feed on animals that she has killed. The kittens learn to hunt by watching her. At six months of age, cougars usually weigh more than 30 pounds (14 kg). They are big and strong enough to start hunting for themselves.

When they are first born, kittens get all the food they need by drinking milk from their mother's body.

Baby cougars are called both kittens and cubs. They are born with dark spots, which help **camouflage** them from predators, such as coyotes and eagles. As cougars grow older, their spots fade.

Time to Move Out

Once the kittens are big enough to begin hunting, the mother will leave her young alone for several days at a time. This forces the kittens to catch their own food. After spending about a year and a half in their mother's territory, the young cougars begin to spread out in search of their own places to live. Scientists call this process **dispersal**.

Cougar kittens play-fight and **stalk** each other. They even wrestle with their mother. These are ways for the young cats to practice the skills they will need to be successful hunters.

These kittens are playing and learning at the same time.

The search for a territory is a dangerous time for cougars. They are still not expert hunters, which means finding food can be hard. Also, as cougar populations grow, it can be harder and harder for cougars to find an area that is not already being used by another cougar. When two cougars want the same territory, they will often fight for it. These battles can result in the death of one of the cougars.

Cougars Moving East

The search for territory may get even harder for cougars in the future. "The cougar population has grown in the West—and so has the human population," explains Clay Nielsen, a wildlife biologist who studies cougar **expansion** eastward. "People are building houses in cougar habitat." The result is that cougars are running out of room in the West.

This cougar walks past a home that was built near the animal's territory in Montana.

In their search for new territory, cougars seem to be moving east. In recent years, there have been more than 300 **confirmed** sightings of the animal in Midwestern states such as Minnesota, Iowa, and Illinois. These are almost always cougars that have traveled hundreds of miles in search of a territory of their own.

Many people think that cats can't swim—but cougars are excellent swimmers. This skill allows them to go farther in search of territories, since they can cross large rivers and other bodies of water.

Even wide rivers, like the Mississippi River, don't stop young cougars in their search for territories. Cougars can swim across rivers, or they can cross them in winter when the water is frozen.

A Long Way from Home

Just how far will young cougars go in search of territory? Amazingly, they have traveled all the way to the East Coast. On June 5, 2011, several people in Greenwich, Connecticut, told police they saw a cougar in the city. Wildlife officials were sure people had seen some other animal. After all, there had been no cougars in Connecticut since the 1880s.

This photo shows a cougar moving east through Wisconsin in early 2010. Scientists believe this is the same cougar that later showed up in Connecticut.

The **witnesses** were not wrong, however. Sadly, just a week after the sightings, the cougar was hit and killed by a car on a Connecticut highway. The cougar was a young male, about two or three years old. Scientists tested the cougar's **genes** to try to figure out where he had come from. The tests showed that the young cougar belonged to a population of cougars living in the Black Hills of South Dakota, which is 1,500 miles (2,414 km) away.

The cougar in Connecticut after it was hit by a car

It's normal for young males to travel up to 100 miles (161 km) to search for a territory of their own or a mate. The trip by the Connecticut cougar, however, is the longest ever observed by scientists. They don't know why the cougar traveled so far, but they believe he was searching for a mate.

Roads are one of the main dangers facing cougars today. The wild cats can be killed trying to cross them. In addition, when cougars are unable to cross roads, they can't reach new habitats or find a mate.

NEXT 2 MILES

Was That a Cougar?

Will cougars continue to spread out from west to east? Clay Nielsen thinks they probably will. "Cougars have the amazing ability to travel hundreds of miles," he says. "They don't know where they are, or where the prey is, but they can keep themselves alive."

Animal Tracks

cougar

dog

coyote

different from those of other

In fact, some people believe there are already cougars living in the Northeast. In the Adirondack Mountains of New York, hundreds of cougar sightings have been reported. Biologists are not convinced, however, without more proof. They say most cougar sightings turn out to be cases of mistaken identity. For example, bobcats are medium-size wild cats that look similar to cougars. As a result, they are sometimes mistaken for their larger relatives.

In order for cougars to breed and form stable populations in places like the Adirondacks, both male and female cougars will have to move east. Scientists, however, are not sure whether this will happen.

Bobcats are smaller than cougars, with pointed ears, shorter tails, and spots on their coats.

Endangered in Florida

There's at least one place in the East that scientists are sure cougars live—southern Florida. Known as Florida panthers, these relatives of the western cougar once lived all over the Southeast. Hunting and habitat loss caused their numbers to drop to around 30 or 40 animals in the 1990s. Today, Florida panthers are still an **endangered species**, with between 100 and 160 panthers living in the wild.

A Florida panther with a deer it has killed

Florida panthers live in Everglades National Park and other park areas of south Florida. They hunt mainly deer and wild hogs, but they will also catch armadillos, raccoons, birds, and even small alligators.

This map shows where Florida panthers lived before the 1800s and where they live today.

Florida Panthers in the Wild: Then and Now

Tennessee

Arkansas

South Carolina

Mississippi

Georgia

Alabama

Atlantic Ocean

Louisiana

Gulf of Mexico

Florida

N
W — E
S

☐ Where Florida panthers lived before the 1800s

■ Where Florida panthers live today

With so few panthers left, scientists are working hard to save every single one. In September 2011, biologists in Florida found two young kittens **orphaned** by the death of their mother. Kittens cannot survive alone in the wild, so the scientists carefully trapped them and took them to the White Oak Conservation Center. Here, the cats can be raised and taught to hunt. Losing the mother was sad, said biologist Darrell Land. "But we hope we can finish the job she started by raising her kittens so they can be returned to the wild."

Florida panther kittens in the wild

Living with Cougars

Scientists believe there are more cougars in the United States today than at any time in the last 100 years. At the same time, cougar habitat is shrinking as cities and **suburbs** continue to expand. Cougar expert Steve Torres says that it's not clear what this will mean for the future of cougars in this country.

This cougar wandered into downtown Santa Fe, New Mexico. It was captured and returned to the wild.

Will it become more common for people to see cougars in the West? Will the search for territory lead cougars to establish new populations in the Midwest and East? "The exciting thing is that we still don't know," said Steve. Cougars are secretive cats, and that makes it hard for scientists to know where they might show up next!

The main threat facing cougars today is habitat loss, due to expanding human populations.

While some people find cougars frightening, in the last 100 years only 14 people in North America were killed by cougars. During that same period of time, more than 15,000 people were killed by lightning, 4,000 by bee stings, and 1,300 by rattlesnake bites.

27

Cougar Facts

The cougar is the largest wild cat in the United States. Here are some other facts about this animal.

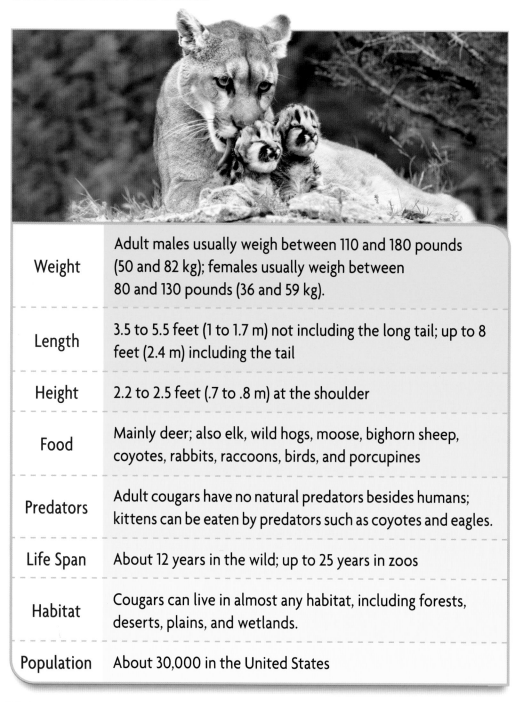

Weight	Adult males usually weigh between 110 and 180 pounds (50 and 82 kg); females usually weigh between 80 and 130 pounds (36 and 59 kg).
Length	3.5 to 5.5 feet (1 to 1.7 m) not including the long tail; up to 8 feet (2.4 m) including the tail
Height	2.2 to 2.5 feet (.7 to .8 m) at the shoulder
Food	Mainly deer; also elk, wild hogs, moose, bighorn sheep, coyotes, rabbits, raccoons, birds, and porcupines
Predators	Adult cougars have no natural predators besides humans; kittens can be eaten by predators such as coyotes and eagles.
Life Span	About 12 years in the wild; up to 25 years in zoos
Habitat	Cougars can live in almost any habitat, including forests, deserts, plains, and wetlands.
Population	About 30,000 in the United States

People Helping Cougars

Humans are responsible for the main threat facing cougars today—loss of habitat. At the same time, however, many people are working hard to save cougars and preserve the habitat they need. Here are two organizations that are working to help cougars and understand their future in the United States:

The Cougar Fund

- Based in Wyoming, this group works to protect cougars and their habitat throughout North and South America.
- The Cougar Fund teaches children and adults about cougars. Members of the group believe that the more people know about these amazing cats, the more they will want to help save them.
- The group also works with hunters in the western United States, teaching them how to identify female cougars so that they don't shoot them. This is important, because if hunters kill mother cougars, their kittens will not be able to survive on their own.

The Cougar Network

- Led by scientific director Clay Nielsen, the Cougar Network studies cougars and the areas that may become new cougar habitat in the Midwest as well as places farther east.
- Clay believes it is important to figure out where cougars may live in the Midwest in the future, and what routes they may take in search of new territory.

Clay Nielsen holding a bobcat

Glossary

adapt (uh-DAPT) to change over time to survive in an environment or habitat

biologists (bye-OL-uh-jists) scientists who study animals or plants

camouflage (KAM-uh-flahzh) to blend in with one's surroundings because of the colors and markings on one's body

carcass (KAR-kuhss) the body of a dead animal

competed (kuhm-PEE-tuhd) tried to get something that others were also trying to get

confirmed (kuhn-FURMD) proven to be true

den (DEN) a home where wild animals can rest, hide from enemies, and have babies

dispersal (dis-PURS-uhl) the process of spreading out in search of new territory

endangered species (en-DAYN-jurd SPEE-sheez) a kind of animal or plant that is in danger of dying out completely

estimated (ESS-ti-mayt-id) to have figured out the approximate amount of something

expansion (ek-SPAN-shuhn) an increase in the size of something

genes (JEENZ) tiny parts of a person or animal that determine characteristics such as body size and eye color

habitat (HAB-uh-tat) a place in nature where an animal is normally found

instinct (IN-stingkt) something an animal does naturally, without having to learn it

keen (KEEN) very sensitive

litter (LIT-ur) a group of animals, such as puppies or kittens, that are born to the same mother at the same time

livestock (LIVE-stok) animals, such as sheep, chickens, and cows, that are raised on a farm or ranch

mate (MAYT) to come together to have young

nurse (NURSS) to feed a young animal milk that comes from the baby's mother

orphaned (OR-fuhnd) left without parents

population (pop-yuh-LAY-shuhn) the total number of people or a kind of animal living in a place

predators (PRED-uh-turz) animals that hunt other animals for food

prey (PRAY) an animal that is hunted by another animal for food

scarce (SKAIRSS) hard to find

settlers (SET-lurz) people who make their home in a new place

solitary (SOL-uh-tair-ee) living alone

stable (STAY-buhl) firm and steady; not changing

stalk (STAWK) to track and follow something

suburbs (SUHB-urbs) areas of homes and businesses close to a city

territory (TER-uh-tor-ee) an area of land that belongs to an animal

witnesses (WIT-niss-iz) people who tell what they saw

Bibliography

The Cougar Network (http://www.cougarnet.org/)

Defenders of Wildlife (http://www.defenders.org/wildlife_and_habitat/wildlife/mountain_lion.php)

Mountain Lion Foundation (http://www.mountainlion.org/index.asp)

Read More

Caper, William. *Florida Panthers: Struggle for Survival (America's Animal Comebacks).* New York: Bearport (2008).

Markle, Sandra. *Mountain Lions (Animal Predators).* Minneapolis, MN: Lerner Publications (2010).

Read, Tracy C. *Exploring the World of Cougars.* Ontario, Canada: Firefly Books (2011).

Rodriguez, Cindy. *Cougars (Eye to Eye with Endangered Species).* Vero Beach, FL: Rourke (2009).

Learn More Online

To learn more about cougars, visit
www.bearportpublishing.com/AmericasHiddenAnimalTreasures

Index

About the Author

Stephen Person has written many children's books about history, science, and the environment. He's never seen a cougar, but did spot a bobcat in Joshua Tree National Park in California. He lives with his family in Saratoga Springs, New York.